LIGHT OF
AWAKENING

By the author

Prose
Twice is not enough
The Lake of Love
There Is Always Something More

Poetry
Palm Lines
River
Cumbrian Lines: poems born of the lake district
The beautiful Ones have been born
Writing is the Happiness of Sorrow

In Igbo
Mmiri a zoro nwayọ nwayọ

In German
Der Schlaf, aus dem ich wachend träume
Innengart
Das dauerhafte Gedicht

Stories for Children:
Somayinozo's Stories

Che Chidi Chukwumerije
Light of Awakening
Second edition 2015.
First edition 2013 under the pseudonym Aka Teraka
Boxwood Publishing House e.K.

Che Chidi Chukwumerije

LIGHT OF AWAKENING

Poems

...

Boxwood Publishing House, Frankfurt

Table of contents

For a friend
dearer than gold
– Susan Merzouk –

Fields Of Light

In fields of light above this realm
Where sight and sound are one
I chanced upon a little elm
A woman sat upon

From far afar I sharp'd my eyes
To peer good at this sight
And soon came I to see thread-ties
'Tween her and the High Light

She sat so still, she did not stir
Or so it seemed to me
'Til I was no more far, but near
And then began to see

Than in her hand she held a flute
The longest yet I've seen
Which stretched gently until its root
Her small lips was between

And she it was who through her sounds
Was forming all these fields
Of beauteous light where joy abounds
And my heart rapture yields

These fields of light I long have passed
Yet never will forget
That those blessed hills, meads, groves were massed
But through that simple set

Of flute and woman weaving music
Healing broken hearts
And forming fields of light of scenic
Beauty for these parts.

Life Unseen

When I see a flower awaken
What do I see?
A fairy in the making
Another guards her sleep

When I hear the wind howling
What do I hear?
Wind-spirits rounding
Up their children in the air

When I feel the gentle raindrops
What do I feel?
A nixie's friendly touch
Connection upon my cheek

The salamander dances
The flames flicker –
Man alone unbalances
Nature's woven wicker

The gnome lends to the tree
His sturdy character –
Wish that I could again see
Mysteries I faintly remember...

Light Of Awakening

It's not the same when you see nothing
Your thoughts return unaccomplished
Without having found the answers
You sent them out to seek –
Heads hung heavy, low
They gather around you again
Unfructified
Quietly you gaze at each other
They recognise their lameness
You your smallness
Thinking you could send out thoughts
Into the dark
And hope they would find the light
An inner voice is speaking...
I'm listening.
Softly:
Light up the flame within your spirit
It will shed light
Upon your way.

First Nature

I feel you close
All those of you
Who love the rose
Within you too,
When you're near
All is fair
As virtue

When you're gone
Or I the bridge
Have again undone,
Built a ridge,
I forget you,
Call you untrue
And intrigue...

But deep within
My human heart,
Beneath the skin,
Another part
Still remembers
In the fire's embers
Our start.

There's more in nature
Than what we see
Behind your second nature
Search quietly
There'll you'll find
Behind your mind
Your first nature...

The one that feels
The beings unseen
The one that heals

In the worlds between
Every night
Weeps for the Light
Unseen.

I feel you close
All those of you
Who love the rose
Within you too –
I know you're near
I almost hear
And feel you...

A bond of love
Unbreakable
Linked to the Dove
A sacred table -
All those who know
Don't let it show...
The world calls it a Fable.

Forming New Ties

I think it was another thought
I was following
But I thought it was the same
Thought of yesterday

I think it was another dawn
I was awaiting
Another dawn, another one
The fruit of yesterday

I have learnt
That yesterday never goes away
Easily –
It changes form, comes again
Here we go again...

The cricket chirps, I know
Although I hear it not for now
Somehow yes somehow I know
I've lived now long enough
To know how it works.

Longing

When my job is done
Will climb into the boat
Row across the river
The other shore
There where the sun is shinning...
Like the sun, I will rise too
When my job is done.

Those wings that spread
Quietly they swept the wind
The song
To some a song of sorrow
To others of joy –
Some wept
Stared into the future and the past
With quiet thoughtful heavy
Hearts of sorrow
Whispered Goodbye...
Others stretched out their arms
A sigh of relief
A smile of joy
Said
Welcome
Welcome back brother
When my job is done.

No sunrise was ever brighter
No sunset ever deeper, memory's keeper
No heaven bluer
Nothing truer, nothing my love
I love you much
How ever far, how ever long
It is but a passing night
The sun will rise
It will rise

Believe me, it will rise
I know, I have been there
And you too – I see it
In your eyes.
Only this I ask of you:
When you see me again
Remember me.

The bird is hovering, it is never far
Waiting to guide the boat
To a distant shore
When my job is done
The canoe
Gently it rocks
On the river banks
Unceasingly
Rocking my intuition...
Memory
You are a visitor
Soon the river will call you
Whether or not
You've finished your job.

Capsized shortlived shortchanged longlived
Heaven where are you?
Downstream or upstream
Oh, for a breath of air! – Last night
I heard water drumming again, gentle congas
Stepping on my soul...
There is a bird singing in the morning light
Who can describe this haunting melody
Assaults my inner Ear?...
Who can taste these salty tears
Still sleep on
In this restless night?
Wake up, little flame,
Oh awake!...
Now, my love, my sweet love

Know me now
Move me now
Do it now or never

Did we ever work side by side?
So short, this eternity
Yet so sweet
Feel it deep
That's all I ask
I too will be gone – it was a Visit –
When my job is done
My longing longs on...

You in my heart
In my heart
There is a garden
I remember
I long to stride across again
You by my side
Tomorrow or today
Or for ever.

Child, Arise...

I have to be
The father of the child in me
Protect him
Encourage him
Allow him to dare to be
The child that should once have been me.

Kingdom of A Thousand Suns

I have lived here
Once before
I know
Upon the blue mountain
On the island of songs
In the kingdom of a thousand suns.

Ode To The Flower

The lines of this poem
Upon this quiet Hour
Dedicated, each one of them,
To you, my flower

Human beings can be very unjust
Some are dark, some are blind
She teaches me to ever trust
In the victory of love true and kind

She flows with the rhythm silently
Subtly sets the tone
Fulfils something for everybody
Each feels she is their own

She flows, stands, dances, hovers
Softens hunters, strengthens gatherers
She makes Knights of her lovers
Kings of mere gardeners

Defeats the desert in every heart
An oasis all on her own
Awakens new worlds, reawakens that part
Of me that has turned to stone

Be ever on the look-out for her
Like a watchman from his tower
Protect, when you see her; thus will you know her:
She who flows is the flower

She opens her heart for all to drink
Who bear the natural thirst
She expresses what all lovers think
Because she was the first

An irresistible smile is her crown
Radiating unselfishly
She lifts my spirit when I am down
Gives unceasingly

She arrests with quiet dignity
Humbly proud, vulnerable
Salvation of the concept of purity
Accessible but unsoilable

Natural, normal, ordinary
Caring, healing gem
She flows with her lovers' and guardians' story
Encourages, comforts, ennobles them

She awakens tears and gentle smiles
Just by being there
Beautiful above all transient styles
A beauty always and fair

Her lovely whiff, caught from afar
Releaser of the deepest sighs
She is mirror of heaven's star
Lights up my soul and eyes

She's nature's victory over human art
Mightier than pen and sword
Speaks deeply to the human heart
Without saying a word

And has one distinct feminine feature:
In her grace lies her power.
She flows with the currents of nature
That's why she's called the Flower...

The Magic Wand

Once upon a time
A magician turned
Himself into a magic wand
And turned his magic wand
Into himself.

There they go
The magician and his wand.

The Future

The way your friends of today
Speak about their friends of yesterday
Is the way they'll speak about you
To their friends of tomorrow too.

It's easy to read the future
All you have to do is remember the past
Most things stay true to their nature
The first shall be the last

It's always pride that leads to the fall
When people peak 'cause they know it all
The sin that brought an angel down
Beware of it when your heights you crown

Those that swim in every wind
Will fall under the influence of your every whim
But when events keep you far away
Another's mind will bend them its way

And those that always rise again
Or stand when others fall in pain
No-one can say the reason why
Yet, no matter what, they never leave your side

It's easy to read the future
If you know how to read the past
Most things stay true to their chosen nature
The first shall be the last

That's why when an Oak falls
Which long stood undefeated and tall
We feel an odd sadness, vulnerability
Injury upon our sense of stability

It is also the reason why
When a Sinner repents, beyond the Sky
The Angels are moved to their very core
And rejoice like never before...

It's easy to read the future
Too often it mirrors the past
Yet leave a little room for error
For the human heart is vast.

When A Baby Smiles...

A little fairy, a lonely elf
All by herself

Hiding in the fields of blue
Quietly watching you

A little baby in your arms
Falls for her charms

Smiles at her and says to her:
Friend, do you live here?

The years will fly past like a sun
Running from the dawn

The child becomes an adult too
Could be me or you

Will saunter past these fields some day,
Eyes fixed on the way

Sees not the elf, hears not her whisper:
You I remember.

Then falls in love, a child is born
That for which we yearn

The adult wonders what it's saying
And with whom it's playing

Sees not that beings have blessed their home
Where unseen they roam

For oft a fairy close by whiles
When a baby smiles.

We take our walks, babies in arm
        Marvel at their charm

We watch them smile at lonesome grass –
        Energy or mass?

Something arrests their attention
        Seen by them alone

An elf informs them wistfully:
        You too will forget me.

Of The Heart

"No war, no peace," says the warrior, wielder of the sword.
"No justice, no peace," says the philosopher, wielder of the pen.
"No forgiveness, no peace," says the lover, wielder of the heart.

"No negotiation, no peace," says the politician, wielder of diplomacy.
"No prayer, no peace," says the priest, wielder of religion.
"No forgiveness, no peace," says the lover, wielder of the heart.

"No invention, no peace," says the scientist, wielder of formulae.
"No knowledge, no peace," says the scholar, wielder of intellect.
"No forgiveness, no peace," says the lover, wielder of the heart.

"No amnesia, no peace," says the coward, wielder of excuses.
"No memory, no peace," says the historian, wielder of records.
"No forgiveness, no peace," says the lover, wielder of the heart.

"No pretence, no peace," says the actor, wielder of theatrics.
"No harmony, no peace," says the musician, wielder of song.
"No reflection, no peace," says the artist, wielder of images.

"No forgiveness, no peace," says the lover, wielder of the heart.

Dimly

I touch my intuition
Every morning
And at night I remember it
Like a friend from long ago
Far away
On the riverbanks of dawn
I forget what I saw in the soft bright sunlight
Of nightly dreams
Sometimes during the day
It will beat
Like a weak heart
I barely hear, barely feel
Quietly inside
Between conversations of How are you?
How are the revenue figures doing?
Very poorly. Stop. And look into the water
And feel your life
Trying to flow back to you, in little ripples
Of intuitively perceived memory
Of the blue island.

Don't shake your head
And tell me you don't understand
I know you simply don't remember...
But I remember you; dimly
Like a friend from long long ago
Far far away
On a blue island....

Waiting, Aye

I just want to be connected with you again –
I want to know your eyes anew
To know your smile anew
To know your specialness anew –
When?

Seconds – Minutes – Moments – Gone...

Making Music

This guitar I remember
Was once a part of my life
A most tender member
A most precious joint
The soil of the start
The point of the matter
The giver of self, she gave herself up...

This guitar I remember.

Meeting Grounds

Meetings such as these
Can take place anywhere
On streets or in the house of dreams
Or upon open pages
That, beckoning, beckon the words
Out of another heart
And if you want to write a poem
The poem will come to you.

The First Recollections

Do you remember how we met?
It was by chance, wasn't it?
That is, if we were to begin now
To believe in chance...
The chance that came our way –
We took it...
Just one look at it
And we took it –

I remember many beginnings
I remember the start of
Many love stories
But our beginning was indeed special
Because it was simply so natural
And so unaffected
Just like all the poems it has given birth to.

That was our beginning
And that shall be our story
The natural and the unaffected
Missing you breaks my heart
Even already on the first day
Without us together
Nothing o nothing will ever be the same Again.

The Ray

When a flower blossoms
We know
That it has been touched by
The ray

When a woman blossoms
We know
That she has been touched by
The ray

The beautiful ray.
When a writer is touched by
The ray
The whole world blossoms.

People Of Planet Earth

Never look too deep into another person's eyes
Never follow far the trade another person plies
Never question hard the words another person says
Never study long the games another person plays

Never think a king has all it takes to be a king
Never think a singer always has a song to sing
Never think a warrior has a warrior-heart in him
Never think a woman has true purity within

Never expect that your friend considers you his friend
Never expect that your guard will guard you to the end
Never expect that your secrets will be safe with me
Never expect that you can honour your vows truly

Because, my brother, man has turned into a beast of late
Because, my sister, yesterday we wandered out a gate
Because, my dear friend, there's a new colour surrounding us
Because, my friend, people of planet earth have lost the cross.

The Dove

The young maiden requested of the youth at the piano
To teach her how to play that piece he played
He sat her by his side and tenderly began to show
The movements of the fingers to be laid

She went home weeping, but the tears were tears of joy and
bliss
And in her memory the piece played on,
But when she got home, sorrow drew her into its abyss:
Quarrelling brothers used her to trade on;

The night went by and morning dawned and restless she arose
And moved as was her wont to the piano,
Played to unburden heart and mind, but could not shed her
woes
'Til she recalled the piece she'd learned to know.

So she began to play the piece, and peace returned to her
And then a wonder began to unfold:
Soon after she released the tones, there flew a dove, sans fear,
To perch on her window, and twitter bold

Amazed the maiden held her breath and continued to play
And the little dove continued to sing,
But when she changed the tune, to make the mood even more
gay
The strange white dove flew off a-fluttering

"Can it be so?", she asked herself, "That if I play this piece,
The unknown dove will come and sing along?
But any other tune, however full of sprite or bliss,
Will drive her forth again without a song?"

So she began to play again the piece the youth taught her
And verily, verily, it was so:

The singing dove returned unto the window-column clear
But when she changed or stopped, the dove would go...

Now she called a brother inside and, full of raptured joy,
Performed for him this miracle of sound
And not even the untamed heart of this untempered boy
Could resist the magic thus come around.

And so it was, her joy was great, her heart burst beyond
bounds
To experience such unity in life –
Such harmony and true beauty that flowed even from sounds
And conquered every woe and every strife!

A-skipping and a-humming and a-dreaming and a-swaying
The young maiden ran cross-town to the youth
To tell him of this wonder that came to her while a-playing
The music piece he'd taught her in his boothe.

The youth was startled by her tale and refused to believe
For 'twas a tale as strange as strange can be
So she sat down at his piano and that music did weave
And the dove came to them, singing freely...

And then the youth, with wondering eyes, told her a startling
thing:
"This piece is called La Paloma – by jove! –
And La Paloma translated out of its Spanish ring
Would mean in English simply but the Dove."

The Earth Is Not My Home

The earth is not my home
Although she ever seems
To weave fine birds that her heights roam
Like I do in my dreams

The earth is not my home
Although she always tries
To spread bright hues across her dome
Like in my home's blue skies

The earth is not my home.
However hard she plot
To dull my homesickness with foam
She in the end cannot

The earth is not my home
And yet I wander here
And know that when my end is come,
Strange, still I'll shed a tear.

The Long Wait

I cut down one tree while I waited
Yet he came not
So I cut down fifty trees, waiting
But he came not
Before I knew it I had cleared a jungle road
Still he had not appeared
Boredom! Boredom!

I chopped the wood of the felled trees
Constructed a big cart
Complete with tyres
Indeed it was a chariot
Where is he?
I fastened horses to my chariot
Taking my time
Laying emphasis on perfection, strength, beauty
Now I was enjoying the work.

It is interesting
I have quite forgotten him
Suddenly he appeared!
Startled, I made to speak
He silenced me with a movement of his hand
Jumped on the chariot
And sped down the jungle road I had cleared
I barely managed to hang on
To that for which I had impatiently waited
All these years.

Fellow Artist

Catch a song in distant heaven
Write it as a poem
Paint it as a picture
Do anything you want
Just make sure that when the expression of your art
Touches me
I'll hear in my heart that first magic
That moved you to do it.

A Bird From An Alien Country

A girl arose from bed one morning
And heard the alien call
Of a bird
From an alien country

She looked out of her window
Saw the bird
Hovering in the air, calling...

The girl became confused
For she could strangely understand the bird's song
And yet knew not its meaning:
> *The first person to trust me*
> *Is mine...*
>> *Sang the bird.*

And then the girl's brother shed his night-gown
And flew out to meet the calling bird – the bird
From an alien country...
And the girl watched them fly away
Two identical birds
To their alien country

The first one to trust me
Is mine.

Ticks Simplicity

There's a ticking in our hearts
Tick-tock-tick-tock
To be simple is an art
One under lock.

The Corpse-Candle

Raki saw the light, a candleflame, coming from the front door
It floated over the ground, over the wall
Into the graveyard, tombstones and all
She remembered Grandpa's words to her this evening upon the moor
"Lass, it's been heaven, these last years with thee,
But now I sense the Call: Death will soon claim me."

Raki's heard the legend all her life, whispered and never loud:
When death will call upon the dying folk
Then life will play his one last joke:
A light emerges from the home of them whom death will soon shroud
Seen only by a few it floats right to there
Where the fated corpse will soon be buried unaware.

Grandpa walked into the house first, while Raki paused outside
And just after the old man entered, Raki saw
A corpse-candle come floating out their door;
So it's really true what folks have known since ages far and wide:
This odd feeling inside her soul is telling Raki
Her time indeed has come to walk eternity.

And so it was with weeping heart Grandpa discovered Raki
Dead the next morning, bitten by a snake
And seeing her corpse his old heart did break.
Lifeless dropped he too beside her, and immortality
Received them both with a gentle smile
That together they may walk the heavenly mile.

Endings

You seek them at the beginnings
And find them not
You seek them through the middles
And find them not
You seek them at the endings
And find them not
Because where you were sure you would meet the End
You met only a new Beginning

And when you have started afresh
You understand that there are no endings
Because no stranger ever affects one so strangely
Or passes one by so quietly
As the end.

Autumn

The leaves become yellow and red
And all those lovely tones in between
There was a gold flame dancing
To a cold wind
When strong fingers held me
And we made that poetry which is music
Because Autumn has reawakened in my heart
And it is a strange feeling
When you are a pen
To be made a Bridge by those who were Bridges
Long before you.

The Return

A boy gave to a girl
A string of promises
Each vow was a pearl
And he strung eleven pearls together
On a silver cord
And presented them to her
As a parting gift…

But those who sow must reap.

She gave his string of pearls
To the man she really loved
And he gave it to the woman
He really loved
She gave it to the person
She really loved
Who gave it to the one
Most truly beloved
And so on and on
Until one day
The boy's string of promises
Found its way
Back to him
Unbroken.

The Marriage

A woman loved a man
And a man loved a woman
They vowed the sacred vow:
Marriage.

Then the woman balked and
Suddenly decided to ask her brother
First... -
She asked him
And he promised to give her the answer
The next day
For he was baffled by the question.

Then he went to a wise man
And questioned him thus:
"Please, Sir, if your sister asks you whether
She ought to marry a man whom
She says she loves,
What would you tell her?"

The sage studied the man's features thoughtfully
For a while, then with an introspective look
Said:
"I would tell her not to marry him."

"What reason would you give her for this, Sir?"

"Truly, I would give her anything
But the true reason,
For that would render it meaningless."

"And what, Sir, is the true reason?"

"Marriage is a sacred, mysterious bond which,

Once taken,
Is embedded forever in the eternal Silence!
It therefore concerns only three:
The man, the woman and the Creator!
Once one of these two humans
Requires the opinion of a third human
To take this step
Then he or she is not yet ready
For Marriage!"

And so, the next day
When the man's sister came for an answer
He told her mysteriously
Wisely nodding his head:
"My sister, in your best interest
I advice you not to marry
Your fiancé.
But ask me not why. Just believe me."

She became destabilized and confused, very...
For she loved her fiancé
Excruciatingly.

But she had her own restless, defiant sage
In her own heart too;
And she decided that her brother was wrong
She went ahead and married her loved one
Resolutely, calmly
Proudly.
Wondering how she could ever have doubted
Or asked a third person,
A stranger to their love.

Invited to her wedding soon after
Her surprised brother,
On arriving
And meeting her fiancé for the first time,
Suddenly became deeply confused...

And now he addressed his sister's laughing husband again:
"You?... You!
Incredible!
But I thought you told me
To tell my sister not to marry you?"

But the sage laughed
And said
In a voice full of respect:
"It turns out that my wife
In the end
Believed her heart
More than she believed the words
Of the forbidden third human...
Because she loves me."

And, so saying,
The young sage went home joyfully
With his wise new wife.

Miracles

Stories.
Like the one about the sad horse
Who came upon a silver lake
And assuaged her thirst.
Tomorrow she will wake up
To suddenly find that
She has begun to sprout wings
Yet she will turn into an eagle
But will remain a horse
Even after her wings gave matured
Because sometimes
Horses are permitted to own their own wings
If they will fly up to there
As hoped
And not just fly down to there
As feared...

I believe
In horses with wings
In fairies that, unobserved, observe us
In animals that can read the thoughts of humans
In babies that knew their own names
Even before they were born
In love that does not die.

Stories.
Like the one about
Two children who climbed
An old tree
And, when they came down,
Had already become adults again.
Tomorrow they will
Become children for a second time
The children they were
First meant to be.

Stories. Stories. Stories.

I believe in miracles
I believe I can fly
I believe in you, baby
Love is a miracle of life.

Stories.
Like the Oracle
That predicted its own demise
And did not bother waiting
To see whether its prediction came true or not.
Stories.
Like the three sisters
Who did not remember they were sisters
Until after they had all fallen in love
With the same man.
Stories. Stories.
Like the creation of the world
Like the adventures of the sojourning stars
Like the mysteries in the wombs of the earth
Like the tired old widow who
Came upon a wishing-well and
After gratefully satiating her thirst
Flipped a coin
And wished the wishing-well well...
Stories.
Like the refugee
Who asked for just a little water and bread
And got it not
Yet could not figure out how to hate.
Stories.
Mysteries.
Oracles.
Miracles.

Everybody

Has a history
But some histories
Are outside everybody.

If you were to behold a miracle
Now,
Would you recognize it as one?
Probably not.

Miracles
Follow me
From life to life
Place to place
Face to face.

There is a Green Hill far away
Once upon a time...
Love.
There is a miracle called love.

Thirty days to Christmas
And here I am
Writing poems
And thinking only of you, my dear.

More Reflections

I see my fears
Reflected in your eyes
And know that your fears
Are mine

I see my home
Reflected off your hands
And know that your home
Is my land

I hear my questions
Echoed in your words
And know that your questions
Are mine

My heart reflects your heart
Your heart reflects my heart
So how many hearts are between us?
How many isles? How many colours?
Four, three, two or one?
Never less.

The Adamantine Spirit Of Lovers

The City!
Somebody called it the
Concrete-Jungle
Hit the nail on the head.

Or should I also call it
The Concrete-Desert?
Or the Ocean of Concrete and Steel
And little warmth?
It is indeed a mocking dragon!
But conquer it aright and you
Would have made it into the
Concrete-Mountain
Braved, crowned and left
Behind...

Look at nature
There is nothing that can match it
Some hearts are made of concrete stone
Some hearts are made of iron and steel
But adamantine is the heart
Of water.

The Lake, The Mountain And The Fountain

Painful inerasable memories
Like a companion dogging my footsteps
And yet one of those mysteries
Is that they don't punch me to those depths
Where the mountain reigns supreme
Waiting for me when I redeem...

In every soul there is a mountain
Before which rests the lake of pain
Upon the mountain there sings a fountain
That maketh spirit whole again
But first you have to cross the lake
Then climb the mountain and now life take.

The Lizard

A few minutes in the garden
Shielded by the trees from
The hot sun
Cooled down by the air cooled by
The greens
And the breezes travelling by
Listening in to the march of Creation
Then the little lizard
Appeared...

It darted forward an inch or two
Then stopped
And nodded in positive affirmation to itself
It darted forward again
Again and again
Nodding each time it stopped
At the gate it paused
And regarded its surroundings
Left, right, even peering beneath the metal
Of the gate

I distinctly perceived a conscious intelligence
Emanating from its movements
A certain wisdom in its jerky swivelling
Face... wide staring eyes
Unsmiling wide-curving mouth
I wondered what it was
Thinking about
Why it was so serious, so alert
In this garden empty of all human presence
But the poet in me...

Again the brown patchy lizard peered
Beneath the locked gate
And then, without a nod,

It slipped out...
For a second I still saw its tail
Then that too was gone

And it had struck me
That that creature had its own life
Its own life-cycle
Its own hopes, its own home
It had had its own childhood
And, one day, in the course of its own activity
Would also depart the flesh
Depart the earth

And whether it was known or acknowledged
Or loved by mankind
Or not
Is beside the point
The point is that it came
It lived
It fulfilled
And it left.

The Wolf Of The Dawn

Sometimes
When the full moon
Is still visible at morning
And the first cockcrows are unheard
Sometimes
When the mist floats
Eerily upon the cold streets
And upon the fields and hilltops
Sometimes
When the sun hesitates
Awhile in shooting out his early rays
And the clouds hasten away from the skies
Sometimes
When sleep is already fading
Although the awakening is still barely underway
And we unconsciously reminisce our stranger dreams

Softly
The birdcall dies away
Softly
The birdcall dies away
And the cattle refuse to stir

Because he is there
The wolf of the dawn

Those who have ears
Hear him breathing
Hear his heart beating out
His lonely howls
Those who have eyes
See him appear and disappear
In the mist
His steady eyes aglow
Sometimes he walks down the street

Sometimes he deposits a paw-mark here
A lingering scent there
He is the wolf of the dawn

He comes... he goes...
And just before he vanishes
On the hilltop
He exchanges a glance with the morning moon
And he howls...

Who will be my friend?

River, River, Flowing Home

I saw a departed soul
There
On the other side of the river
Yet there was no bridge
Across the river...
So how did he get there?
How did he cross to the other
Side of the river...?

River, river, flowing home
River, river, flowing home

Bathed in the mild glows of
The fields across
The river
Stood a soul
And he said Brother
Goodbye...

River, river, flowing home
River, river, flowing home

For Kwame

Two Roads That Never Meet

In space, so strange, I observed
That roads abound
Some straight, some crooked, some even swerved
And came around
And then saw I two roads together walking
Side by side they walked, all the while talking

They spoke, they joked, they conversed
But never touched
Ye still as friends they traversed
Countries that notched
They sometimes turned and peered into each other's eyes
And yet, so strange, they never formed any ties

They diverged, they converged, and again,
For days on days
They changed, they exchanged, each its lane
Yet kept their ways
And on and on they travel on their way to Heaven
Never parting, never touching, sometimes odd, always even...

The Singularity Of Every

There are many things
That seem to be the same
But are not
Just like dawn and dusk
Who have a way of appearing similar
And yet have never met
Or seen
Nor ever will
Nor ever be the same.

The Avenger

In the first age
When man and nature rode a common will
I saw the shadow of the Avenger in the cool
Standing still

In the second age
When man ate the apple and the flood ate him
I saw the shadow of the Avenger in the cool
Looking grim

In the third age
When wise teachers tried to change man
I saw the shadow of the Avenger in the cool
Dead-pan

In the fourth age
When man refused to heed a stream of prophets
I saw the shadow of the Avenger in the cool
He never frets

In the fifth age
When Love came to man and man killed Him
I sought the shadow of the Avenger in the cool
And all was dim

In the sixth age
When man wantonly stole fruits he never farmed
I saw the shadow of the Avenger in the cool
Fully armed

Now it's the seventh age
I see man frantically trying to flee the hot sun
The light rays of the Avenger burn too brightly
For It has begun.

May Song

The children come out to play
And all is gay
In the month of May.

The farmers make their hay
In the shinning sun's ray.

Hand in hand as they go their way
Young lovers whisper what they have to say
On their way to hear the new priest pray.

And following the song of the stock-bird jay
Gentle old couples of yesterday
Quietly remember their youth today.

The essentials will stay
When all else goes away.

This is the song in the heart of May.

A Flower In May

What colour is that tone of blue?
Who, baby, exactly are you?
I almost know but ignorant stay
And now must be on my way.

At the site at the end of the journey
Animals with skin hard, horny, corny
People with intentions noble and fair
Battling the growth that eats into everywhere.

A flower in May, the Children's Day
We drive out along Kaduna's Way...
The cycle completes, I'm back again
To search again for the rhyme again...

What tone exactly is that evening blue?
Different from the morning's azure hue
What marks each person out? What makes
Me me, you you, different souls, different lakes?

The Hidden Feather

The hidden feather
There and not there
Fluttering silent soft
Bearing a great thing aloft.

Being genuine.

A foolish student
Will one day become a wise teacher
An unyielding sinner
Will one day become a moving preacher
The gap that yawns in you today
Will be filled by the pain of growth
Perfection and Imperfection may look like opposites
But when they arise in you, embrace them both
Because you don't know which is which
Who is really poor and who is really rich.

Four Seasons Later

First we greet the Spring
Marching into May
With April in our Hearts...
Bushes, bursting full like joy-filled hearts
With the yellow, red and orange
Of torch-lilies
The velvety beige-red of strong little roses
And something blue everywhere...

The uncut grass will sway
Because a gentle wind, a singing heart is throbbing, bursting
Like a basket of wild berries –
Water fills the air
From up it comes down
The earth is green and overflowing
With life, raining, running
Overflowing...

It is the water that takes over
Until November
Or even December –
I progress beside yon Marina
Lagoon by my side
Waterways
Streams like streets and highways
Motorways for the hearts a-flowing...

And, morning a-swaying
All I see upon the water
A white blanket, soft, chalk
From heaven to sea-lagoon-river-stream-water
Is the same dreamy Haze from four subtle seasons ago, I
Smell it, I smell her, coming
Again, come again,
The harmattan.

Cherished Times

The end is always hard
Who can part
With the scene of his true living?
We spend our lives dying
If ever we did anywhere anytime
For a moment live
Who can with this moment part
From this scene depart
Without a tear?

Just Dance

A road of water, slippery
A bridge of knife-edge, treacherous
A fall of repetition, weakening
An opacity of reflection, saddening
A backdoor of wall, illusionary
A tiger if library, jealous
A conscience of intuition, merciless
Hardfall on softpain, intangibles
Awakening twice, once to life and once to self
Accepting the conditions of the journey
Intangibles, contradictions, repetitions, unpredictables
Armed with Intuition and intellect
Go with the flow.

Pain

If you avoid pain, you avoid life
If you avoid life, you avoid youth
If you avoid youth, you avoid love
If you avoid love, you avoid experiencing
If you avoid experiencing, you avoid growth
If you avoid growth, you avoid change
If you avoid change, you avoid strength
If you avoid strength, you avoid happiness
If you avoid happiness, you avoid disappointment
If you avoid disappointment, you avoid movement
If you avoid movement, you avoid knowledge
If you avoid knowledge, you avoid yourself
If you avoid yourself, you avoid beauty
If you avoid beauty, you avoid life...
Do not fear Pain. It is the proof that you live,
The outgrowing of yourself
The door that separates you from your dreams.
Cross it.
The acceptance, experiencing and mastering of pain
Is the seed out of which the tree of life shall blossom
In all its rich manifestation...
For you.

Magical Moment

If we could see the future, what would be its past?

If we could see the future, would we change the present?
And would we then see the new future that arises out of that?

If we could see the future, would it still be the future,
or would we have turned it into the past?

And what would the future then be?

I guess we can never really see the future...
The present is the future.

Authority Within

There is a poet
He lives in me
I am his host and his prisoner –

He is not married to my wife
He is not related to my family members
He does not come from my country
He does not work for my employer
He is a recluse
A hermit
Who lurks sometimes seen sometimes unseen
In the waters within my heart
I heard his name
They called him Spirit.

He looks at me
With his burning eyes
Only when he has something to say
Then, calling my name, he commands:
"Pen, write..."
And I write.
And that's all I know about him.

Music Forever

I wonder
How it will be
On the day I die –
Will I hear that music?

This whole journey
What has it been worth
If I don't hear that music?

If tomorrow
Will unteach me how to hear that music
Then take me today, dear Lord...
If today I am still deaf
To that music
Then guide me to the source
Of that guitar, and teach me how to grasp
Thine song, Lord, before my day
Is come.

As empty as life is
Even emptier is death
Without music.

Renewal

Every end is a bend
Every conclusion is a transition
Every termination is a transformation
The terminal is diurnal
Life means undeath
Unsheathe the wreath
Catch your eternal breath
My friend.

Love

Simple Simon
made a rhyme on
something on his mind:

If God is love,
all else above,
then how can love be blind?

January Is Dawn

The Christmas holiday season
is like a dream

In January you wake up and
try to retain

as much of the dream as possible
within your heart.

www.ingramcontent.com/pod-product-compliance
Lightning Source LLC
Chambersburg PA
CBHW020517030426
42337CB00011B/440